WHAT MAKES IT RAIN?

Susan Mayes

Designed by Mike Pringle
Illustrated by Richard Deverell and Mike Pringle

Series editor: Heather Amery

CONTENTS

All about rain

When grey clouds start to fill the sky, this often means that rain is on the way.

The rainwater runs down drains, or into streams, rivers and lakes. Some of it makes puddles on the ground.

Sometimes there is too much rain and sometimes there is not enough. When the air is cold snow may fall.

When the rain stops and the sun comes out, puddles on the ground get smaller and smaller.

Where does the water go when it dries up? How does water get into the sky to make more rain?

What is a weather forecast and how is it made? You can find out about all of these things in this book.

Where the water goes

After a shower of rain, heat from the sun begins to dry up all the water on the ground.

The water turns into tiny droplets in the air, leaving the ground dry. The droplets are so small that you cannot see them. They are called water vapour.

When water dries up, this is called evaporation.

Try this

On a hot day, try this experiment to make water dry up.

Put two plates in a sunny place with a spoonful of water in each one.

Shade one plate with a book.

Look at the plates every hour.

Heating up

If a pan without a lid boils on a high heat for a long time, the water will evaporate and the food burns.

The water in the sun dries up first. Water always evaporates more quickly in the hot sun than it does in the cool shade.

4

Warm air

When air is warmed, it rises. You cannot see it moving, but you can sometimes see how it takes things up, high into the sky.

Smoke from a fire rises up the chimney and into the sky.

Warm air from a bonfire carries sparks and bits of ash upwards.

Try this

Hold a very thin piece of tissue paper over a heater.

The air warmed by the heater rises and lifts the paper.

The sun's heat

Warm air and water vapour.

Air rises when it is warmed by the sun. It carries water vapour from the land and sea up into the sky.

Water in the air

When water vapour in the air cools, it turns into water drops which you can see. This is called condensation.

Your warm, damp breath makes steamy clouds on a cold day.

Steam from hot water is water vapour which has turned into tiny drops in the cold air.

Try this

Breathe hard on a cold mirror and see what happens.

The water vapour in your breath collects on the mirror and makes it mist up.

Did you know?

You can sometimes see water vapour very high in the sky behind aeroplanes.

It is pushed out of the engines and leaves long trails of white cloud in the cold air.

Dew

On a warm day there is a lot of water vapour in the air. This is because warm air can hold more water vapour than cold air.

As the warm air cools down at night, some of its water vapour condenses. It turns into water drops on leaves and cool ground.

These water drops are called dew. You can see it on the ground in the early morning. The sun soon dries it up.

Frost

If the air gets very cold at night, dew freezes into frost.

Fog

Sometimes it is so cold that dew does not form. Water vapour condenses straight into frost.

Frost is often so thick and white that it looks like a covering of snow on the ground.

Fog is lots of tiny water drops in the air. The drops form when air full of water vapour cools near the ground.

7

Cold air

The heat from the sun bounces off the ground and warms the air near it. The air higher up in the sky is much colder. It is so cold that high mountain tops are snowy all year.

How clouds form

Every day water from the sea evaporates in the sun.

The warm air near the ground carries the water vapour up into the sky.

The cold air makes the water vapour condense into groups of tiny drops or ice crystals. We see them as clouds.

Did you know?

In some parts of the world people can sunbathe on a beach and see snow on the high mountains.

8

Above the clouds

When you take off in an aeroplane, you can go through the clouds and fly above them. The sun shines up there all the time during the day.

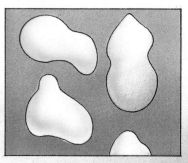

Inside a cloud

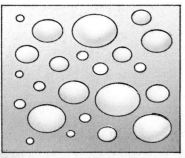

The millions of tiny water droplets which make a rain cloud are different sizes.

Big drops fall and bump into smaller ones. They join and make bigger drops.

When the water drops are heavy enough they fall to Earth as drops of rain.

Below the clouds

The rainwater collects in seas, lakes, rivers and puddles. When it stops raining the sun will start to dry up this water.

9

Snowy weather

How snowflakes form

Most water drops in high clouds freeze into tiny specks of ice in the cold air.

As they fall, more water freezes on them. They become ice crystals.

When the crystals are big enough, they join together and fall as snowflakes.

Falling snowflakes soften in warmer air. They stick together easily. Sticky snow makes good snowballs.

Snowflake facts

All snowflakes are a six-sided shape.

Millions of snowflakes have fallen to Earth, but nobody has ever found two which are exactly the same.

Did you know?

People have seen huge snowflakes the size of large plates.

Avalanches

A skier or a loud noise can start an avalanche.

An avalanche is lots of snow which slides down a steep mountain slope. This may happen when the weather gets warmer and snow starts to melt.

Hail

Hailstones are hard lumps of ice which form inside a storm cloud. They fall to the ground very quickly in a hailstorm.

Raindrops freeze into ice pellets at the top of a storm cloud.

Air currents toss them up and down. More water freezes on to them.

When the pellets are too heavy to stay up, they fall as hailstones.

Inside a hailstone

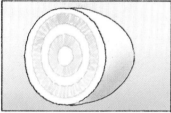

If you cut a hailstone you would see the layers of frozen water.

Did you know?

The biggest hailstone ever found was 19cm across, which is nearly as big as a football.

Hailstone damage

Big hailstones can make dents in cars and break windows. A bad hailstorm can flatten a field of corn in just a few minutes.

Rainbows

Next time it rains and the sun is shining at the same time, look for a rainbow.

How a rainbow is made

A ray of light looks white but it is really made up of many colours.

When sun shines through a raindrop the water splits the light into all its colours.

sunlight

raindrop

The colours bounce off the back of the drop and bend as they come out.

Rainbow colours

There are seven main colours in a rainbow and they are always in the same order – red, orange, yellow, green, blue, indigo and violet.

Try this

Put a glass of water on a sheet of white paper. Make sure it is in front of a sunny window.

When the sun shines brightly, a small rainbow will appear on the paper.

A rainbow appears when sunlight shines on falling drops of water in a waterfall.

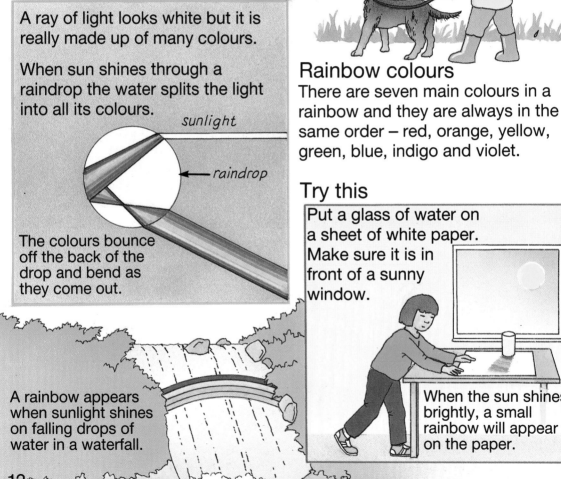

Thunderstorms

Tall, dark clouds often bring a storm with thunder and flashes of lightning.

What is lightning?

A kind of electricity, called static electricity, starts to build up in a storm cloud.

When there is too much, it jumps from the cloud in a huge, hot spark. This spark is the flash of lightning which you see in the sky.

Why we hear thunder

A flash of lightning heats the air around it very quickly. It starts a huge wave of air which grows bigger and bigger. This makes the thunder which you hear.

Lightning can go from cloud to cloud, or from the cloud down to the ground.

Try this

Make your own spark of static electricity.

Press a large lump of plasticine on to a tin tray to make a handle.

Hold the plasticine and rub the tray round and round on top of a thick plastic bag.

Hold something metal near the corner of the tray. Watch a spark jump away.

13

Water on the ground

In a town, rainwater runs down the drains. It is carried away by underground pipes.

In the country, rainwater runs down slopes and into streams, rivers and lakes. Some soaks into the ground.

As a stream flows along, it is joined by more water from springs and from under the ground.

A river finds the easiest way across the land.

The water trickles down through the soil. It goes into underground streams and wells, then it travels on under the ground.

Sometimes underground water comes out of the side of a hill as a spring. Most streams start from a spring in this way.

Snow and ice melt when the weather warms up. The water runs away and soaks into the ground.

As the rivers, streams and springs make their way to the sea, some of their water evaporates.

More streams join together and they form a river.

A small river which flows into a bigger one is called a tributary.

Some water collects in hollows in the ground. This is how lakes are formed.

The river mouth is where the water runs out into the sea and ends its journey.

Water evaporates from the sea every day. The tiny invisible droplets will soon collect to make more clouds.

Too much rain

A flood sometimes happens when there is a very heavy rainstorm, or if it rains for a long time. The water cannot all seep away into the ground and it runs on to the land. Streams and rivers overflow with water.

Snow and ice

Floods sometimes happen in the spring when snow and ice start to melt. The water cannot soak into the soil because the ground is still frozen hard underneath.

Stopping the water

A dam is a wall which is built across a river to make a lake. It holds the water back and can also be used to control floods.

A sudden flood

A flood which happens very suddenly is called a flash flood. It happens when a huge amount of rain falls in one place in a very short time.

There was a flash flood in New South Wales, Australia, in April 1989. The water swept away roads, bridges, cars, buildings and animals.

Living with rain

People in Indonesia build houses on stilts. They will be safe above the water when the floods come.

Moving away

The people of Barotseland, Zambia, move away when the floodwaters come. They take all their belongings to higher ground.

The driest places

Drought

In some places it does not rain for many weeks. There is not enough water to drink or grow plants. This dry time is called a drought.

Did you know?

A strange plant grows in Africa's Namib Desert. Its leaves soak up water vapour from fog and it lives for at least a thousand years.

Deserts are the driest places in the world. In some places it does not rain for years. Any water evaporates quickly in the hot sunshine.

Cacti are desert plants which store the water they need in their stems.

In the United States, water from the Colorado River runs along canals to the Sonoran Desert. It is pumped on to the dry land to grow crops.

Did you know?

A camel can live for as long as ten days in the desert without drinking.

Its body slowly turns fat in the hump into the water it needs.

The long roots of the mesquite plant find water 53 metres down under the ground.

Kangaroo rats never drink. Their bodies have a special way of making water from the dry seeds which they eat.

Desert flowers

Seeds of flowers lie in the dry soil waiting for rain. When it falls, the flowers bloom very quickly but they only live for a day or two.

What kind of weather?

A weather forecast tells you what the weather is going to be like. You can see it on television, hear it on the radio or read it in the newspaper.

Weather forecasts can help you decide what to wear or where to go for the day.

People who need to know

An aircraft pilot needs to know what the weather will be like on the flight.

A fisherman needs to know if the weather at sea is going to be fine or stormy.

A farmer uses weather forecasts every day. He needs good weather for a lot of his work.

Making a weather forecast

A weather station is where facts about the weather are collected at certain times every day.

More facts come from satellites which study the weather from space.

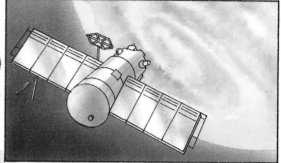

They measure the wind speed and the water vapour in the air. They even measure the temperature.

Forecasters collect facts from weather stations around the world and from satellites. They use the facts to make weather charts.

They use these charts to help make a weather forecast. This tells you what the weather will be like over the next few days.

Useful words

You can find all of these words in this book. The pictures will help you to remember what the words mean.

canal
This is a special waterway built for ships and to carry water across land.

condensation
This is tiny drops of water you see on cold things. It forms when warm, damp air touches something cold.

dam
This is a wall built to hold water back and make a lake.

desert
This is a dry place, where it hardly ever rains. Only a few plants grow.

dew
This is the name for the small drops of water which form on cool ground, leaves and plants.

evaporate
This is what happens when water dries up. It turns into tiny, invisible water drops in the air.

flood

This is when lots of water covers the land, after too much rain.

frost

This is tiny drops of frozen water which appear on the ground and on other things in cold weather.

hail

This is the name for lumps of ice which form in a storm cloud.

fog

This is tiny drops of water which you can see in the air. It looks like patches of low cloud.

water vapour

This is the name for tiny droplets of water in the air. The droplets are so small you cannot see them.

weather satellite

This is a machine sent into space to study the weather around the Earth.

Index